from grief to peace

from *grief* to *peace*

a guided journal for navigating loss
with compassion and mindfulness

heather stang

CICO BOOKS
LONDON NEW YORK

Published in 2021 by CICO Books
An imprint of Ryland Peters & Small Ltd
20–21 Jockey's Fields   341 E 116th St
London WC1R 4BW   New York, NY 10029

www.rylandpeters.com

10 9 8 7 6 5 4 3 2 1

A CIP catalog record for this book is available from the
Library of Congress and the British Library.

ISBN: 978-1-80065-019-0

Printed in China

Commissioning editor: Kristine Pidkameny
Senior editor: Carmel Edmonds
Senior designer: Emily Breen
Art director: Sally Powell
Head of production: Patricia Harrington
Publishing manager: Penny Craig
Publisher: Cindy Richards

contents

introduction

There is no shortage of people eager to tell you how to cope with grief and loss. However, only one person can honestly know what you need: you. Even though you may not feel like you can hear it, your inner wisdom is already speaking to you. It inspired you to open this journal. A part of you is ready to do something to reduce your suffering and start feeling like yourself again.

I hold a Master's Degree in Thanatology, the study of death, dying, and bereavement, and am a certified Phoenix Rising Yoga Therapist. I facilitate the Awaken Meditation for Grief Online Program through the Mindfulness & Grief Institute and work with local and national bereavement organizations.

I am also a bereaved person who had to find a way to cope with grief. I know firsthand that this is not easy. I also know that with the right tools and the right support, you can do this.

Your grief and loss experience is very personal. There is no single right way to navigate life after loss, and I cannot tell you what to do. What I can do is offer you hope and direction, and empower you to choose the steps you take through mindfulness and journaling.

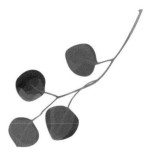

Mindfulness is a meditation style and a mindset rooted in being present and openhearted. Journaling is a style of writing that gives a tangible form to your innermost feelings.

This guided journal has the prompts, inspirations, mindful movement exercises, and expressive art projects to help you get to know yourself better so you can learn how to do more than just cope with loss; you will learn how to live fully with your loss.

loss and grief

You probably picked up this journal intending to focus on one loss in particular. Naturally, some are more painful. A loved one's death is irreversible and is the most distressing for many. This is not true for everyone. For some, the most significant losses in life are not associated with death.

The prompts in this journal will help you explore and integrate all types of loss. The yearning you feel when someone special dies. The anticipatory grief that follows a life-limiting diagnosis. The traumatic grief you feel when someone dies by suicide, an overdose, or an act of violence. The ambiguous losses that leave you feeling anxious, such as a loved one with dementia, a mental health diagnosis, or an estranged family member. And, of course, those losses that matter to you, but are disregarded and minimized by others because they just don't understand.

We are all connected and face collective losses that impact us as a society and as individuals. To heal ourselves, we need to name what hurts and find a way to continue on.

how to use this guided journal

This guided journal is your sacred space, so instead of rules, I offer a few suggestions below.

There are no right or wrong answers.

Let the truth fall onto the page and resist the urge to edit. When you write, keep your pen or pencil moving at a calm and steady pace without stopping until you complete the prompt.

Mindfully engage with your whole being.

Mindful journaling invites you to notice your breath as you write or draw. Feel emotions in your body when you tell the story. Hear the sounds in the room and outside your window as you draw. When you pay attention to your senses as you write, you are writing mindfully.

Approach familiar subjects as if it were the first time.

Mindful journaling frees you from habitual ways of telling your story so you can relate to it differently. When you encounter a prompt that feels familiar, slow down your thinking and writing speed. Be curious and explore the little details that you previously missed. Tap into your beginner's mind.

Walk up to the edge, but don't fall over.

In Phoenix Rising Yoga Therapy, we often talk about finding our edge: that place in a stretch—or an emotion, or in telling your story—that is just right. If you go over the edge, you experience pain. If you don't go far enough, the experience is boring and will not help you move forward. The edge may feel tolerably uncomfortable, or fresh and exciting, but it is never dangerous or harmful. Be mindful of your edge, and adjust your attention to it accordingly to find the right balance.

Seek out physical and emotional support as needed.

Writing in this journal will help you develop coping and self-care skills, but no person is an island. This is especially true when working through grief and loss. Call a friend or a hotline, schedule regular appointments with a therapist, or join a grief group. Grief research shows that social support is one of the key elements to help you adapt to life after loss. Please do not try to do it alone.

Go through the journal in order. Or don't.

Grief is not a linear experience, yet most people experience a similar arc. This guided journal was created with this trajectory in mind. Many people will benefit from going in order, but if you skip around, that is fine too. When you encounter a prompt that you are not ready to answer, you can always move on and return to it later.

Along the way, you will encounter pages marked with a colored border around the edges. These sections contain a bit more guidance before the activities or prompts. If you are feeling stuck, turn to one of these.

If you are focusing on a non-death loss, you may wish to skip pages 96, 100, and 101, which focus on grief specific to the death of a person or pet.

This journal features inspirational quotes at the start of each chapter. These are from my first book (see page 144), which parallels the structure of this guided journal and is a great companion book if you like to read as well as write.

Grief is hard. Whenever you can, be kind to yourself. At the end of the day, this is the most important thing you can do. May this process bring you peace and free you from suffering.

With gratitude,

heather

Your why is more important than your how when it comes to mindfully navigating your grief. Let's begin with both an aspiration to help you get started and a reminder that you may turn to again and again. Take a couple of mindful breaths, write slowly, and answer with your whole heart.

What inspired you to purchase this guided journal, or if it was given to you as a gift, what inspired you to begin?

_____

_____

_____

_____

_____

_____

What do you hope will be different after you complete this guided journal?

_____

_____

_____

_____

_____

Write a few words of encouragement and gratitude to yourself for taking this next step on your journey, even if you are not yet sure where it will take you.

_____

_____

_____

_____

_____

_____

_____

mindfully relating to your grief means being fully aware of your experience of loss while simultaneously embracing whatever arises in you with compassion and loving-kindness.

mindful awareness

When grief has shattered your assumptive world, mindfulness will help you find stability in the present and empower you to choose how you relate to your experience. Freed from habitual ways of thinking, you will see more clearly the next step you need to take on your grief journey.

Connect with the part of you that is **aware that you are aware**.
Note what you sense in your:

breath

body

thoughts

emotions

What one thing stands out to you the most?

_____

_____

_____

_____

_____

Mindfully tending to my grief matters to me because...

Lie down and soften your body as much as possible. Place one hand on your belly, another over your heart. Spend a few moments and several rounds of breath for each item below:

1. Notice your natural breath.
2. Now breathe low and deep into just your belly for a few breaths. Expand your belly on the inhale, release your belly on the exhale.
3. Next, breathe first into your belly, then into your mid-section up to your lower ribs. Exhale and let it go.
4. Fill your belly first, then your mid-section, and finally breathe all the way into your lungs before letting go in a complete exhale.
5. Let go of all effort and rest with natural breath and in mindful awareness. Just be.

Describe the places in your body that feel stuck or tight.

_____

_____

_____

Describe the places in your body that feel open or relaxed.

_____

_____

_____

Are there places in your body that feel neutral or in between?

_____

_____

_____

Your breath is your home base; a safe place to rest your attention.

Mindfulness meditation often uses an object of focus—such as your breath—to stabilize your attention before expanding your awareness to all of your senses. Spend a few minutes focused just on your natural breath. Inhale and exhale without controlling anything other than where you place your attention.

When I pay attention to my natural breath I…

build your resilience toolkit for grief

Two resilience boosters are coping skills and self-care techniques. These will help you feel more at ease in the short term and teach you powerful tools to manage future stress with more confidence than before.

Coping skills are things you can do to reduce feelings of distress in the heat of the moment. Your list might include taking a few deep breaths, counting to 10, going for a walk, listening to your power song, or calling a supportive friend.

Make a list of the difficult emotions and feelings you encounter regularly. Next to each difficult emotion, write down your typical reaction. Ask yourself, is this reaction healthy (skillful) or unhealthy (unskillful) for you in the long term?

Difficult emotion: _____

Typical reaction: _____

Skillful or unskillful? _____

Difficult emotion: _____

Typical reaction: _____

Skillful or unskillful? _____

Difficult emotion: _____

Typical reaction: _____

Skillful or unskillful? _____

Difficult emotion: _____

Typical reaction: _____

Skillful or unskillful? _____

Difficult emotion: _____

Typical reaction: _____

Skillful or unskillful? _____

Difficult emotion: _____

Typical reaction: _____

Skillful or unskillful? _____

For any unskillful reaction on the previous exercise, write down a healthy coping skill that you can do the next time this feeling arises.

When I feel
_____
in the past I reacted by
_____
but now I choose to respond by
_____

When I feel
_____
in the past I reacted by
_____
but now I choose to respond by
_____

When I feel
_____
in the past I reacted by
_____
but now I choose to respond by
_____

Self-care techniques are preventative activities that help you maintain a sense of inner peace and calm while boosting your overall health and wellbeing.

Make a list of daily, weekly, and monthly self-care practices that you can plan to do regularly. Put these on your calendar and commit to regular self-care, knowing it will help you navigate grief and stress with less suffering.

Daily self-care practices:
_____
_____
_____

Weekly self-care practices:
_____
_____
_____

Monthly self-care practices:
_____
_____
_____

Sit comfortably and focus your attention on the sounds in and around you. Allow waves of sound to come and go naturally for at least three minutes. As best you can, resist interpreting or analyzing what you hear. When you become distracted, just start over with the next sound you hear. (You can also replace sound with sight or smell for this exercise).

How does letting go of having to do anything about what you experience change how you relate to the present moment?

Notice what you are...

1. feeling in your body
2. seeing with your eyes
3. hearing with your ears
4. smelling with your nose
5. tasting with your tongue
6. thinking in your mind.

Without seeking out any single sensory input, notice the natural ebb and flow of what you experience. No clinging. No avoidance. Just allowing.

How does **coming to your senses** influence how you feel moment to moment?

_____

_____

_____

_____

_____

_____

_____

_____

_____

_____

_____

_____

_____

_____

_____

_____

_____

_____

_____

_____

There is no right way to grieve. Imagine you could really let go and be really honest with yourself about your grief experience.

Reflect on how grief has impacted your:

Body

Thoughts

Emotions

Behaviors

Relationships

Spiritual beliefs

Worldview

One thing I know to be true in this moment is...

Go for a mindful walk outside (eyes open!). Let the movement of your body keep you grounded in the present moment. When you lose touch with presence, allow your senses to be your gateway back to here and now. After your walk, reflect below.

When I am present in the natural world...

Is grief like the desert? An unending wilderness? The untamed ocean? Maybe grief feels like another planet. Using the concept of a landscape as a metaphor, draw or collage your experience of grief. Include elements such as land, sky, bodies of water, plants, and even buildings or animals.

A closing ritual at the end of each meditation session is a simple way to express gratitude for your wise effort. It is also a reminder that your intention to be present can continue throughout your day. One example is to press your palms together at your heart center as you bow your head slightly in reverence.

How will you close your meditation practice, and what does this symbolize to you?

If you think of your life as a journey, and the present moment is the "You Are Here" marker on the map, where are you now?

Where do you want to be?

we receive messages from our body
when we need to take action. we can
also reverse this process, and send
our body a message.

conscious relaxation

Grief impacts your whole being. Fortunately, the mind-body connection is a two-way street. Focusing your mind will release tension in your body. Tending to your body will ease emotional pain. This practice of conscious relaxation flips your stress switch to off so you can be healthy and resilient now and for years to come.

Below are some of the common symptoms of grief. Check off the ones you have experienced. Add in any other changes you have observed in your physical body since your loss.

☐ Hollowness in the stomach

☐ Tightening of the throat, chest, and stomach

☐ Increased aches and pains

☐ Sleeplessness or sleepiness

☐ Oversensitivity to noise

☐ Shortness of breath and frequent sighing

☐ Lack of energy

☐ Muscle weakness

☐ Dry mouth

☐ Lack of coordination

What other changes to your physical body have you noticed since your loss?

What type of relationship do you have with your body now?

What kind of relationship do you **want** to have with your body?

Slowly scan through and linger on each part of your body. Notice how your bones, muscles, joints, and organs feel right now. When you notice yourself judging, analyzing, or telling yourself a story about your body, come back to your direct experience. When you are finished, use the space below as directed:

1. Draw an outline to represent your body.

2. Use three different colored pens, pencils, or crayons, to shade in the parts where you felt one or more of the three feeling tones—pleasant, unpleasant, and neutral.

Note what stood out to you in your body during this exercise.

Using what you noticed in the body scan, make a plan to befriend your body by taking care of it—or even indulging it—in the coming week.

I will be kind to the parts that feel unpleasant by...

I will celebrate the parts that feel pleasant by...

I will be curious and open to the parts that feel neutral by...

the sleep and rest you need

Although sleep disturbances are expected in the early period of navigating loss, it is essential to try your best to get enough rest. Like taking care of your teeth, good sleep hygiene includes healthy techniques and habits that will set you up for bedtime success. Choose two things from the sleep hygiene list below that you can do every day this week.

- [ ] Exercise during the day

- [ ] Limit caffeine and alcohol

- [ ] Tend to your physical tension

- [ ] Create a relaxing bedroom environment

- [ ] Avoid screen time 1 hour before bed

- [ ] Write down tomorrow's to-do list

- [ ] Meditate, do yoga, or relax before bed

- [ ] Go to bed and wake up on a regular schedule

Keep track of how you do this week on the chart below.

	How did you sleep last night?	How do you feel today?
Day 1		
Day 2		
Day 3		
Day 4		
Day 5		
Day 6		
Day 7		

List the sources of tension and stress in your life that impact your body. Let go of self-judgment as you do this, and include both internal causes, such as worries and regrets, and external causes, such as work stress, or financial concerns.

Internal causes   External causes

---   ---
---   ---
---   ---
---   ---
---   ---
---   ---
---   ---
---   ---
---   ---
---   ---
---   ---
---   ---
---   ---
---   ---
---   ---
---   ---
---   ---

Review the above list:

1. Circle the sources of tension and stress that you can let go of easily.

2. Put a plus next to sources of tension and stress that will require a little more effort to work through, but that you feel can be addressed without too much work.

3. Put a star next to the sources of stress that seem permanent now, but that you feel may change in the future.

The stress response we also call fight-flight-freeze is naturally triggered by our loss experience. Review your list of internal and external sources of stress on page 36 and choose three that you feel have caused the most physical suffering over the past week or two. For each one, describe how your body feels and a way that you can reduce your suffering the next time you experience it.

Source of stress:
How did your body feel?

How can you reduce your suffering next time?

Source of stress:
How did your body feel?

How can you reduce your suffering next time?

Source of stress:
How did your body feel?

How can you reduce your suffering next time?

Source of stress:
How did your body feel?

How can you reduce your suffering next time?

Before your loss, how did you spend your free time?

What did you do to relax?

Make a list of relaxing activities you want to start doing again.

Choose one activity from your list that you can commit to doing this week:

Choose one activity from your list you can commit to doing next month:

What new relaxing activities do you want to try? Commit to taking time to research how to get started and keep a list here.

Relaxing activity	How to get started

Spend 10–30 minutes doing one or a combination of the following:

- Lie on the floor and stretch the places that crave expansion.
- Explore yoga postures without any preconceived ideas of how it "should" look.
- Massage the places in your body that are holding tension.
- Rest your hands on the parts of you that will benefit from extra loving-kindness.

What is different in your body after this experience?

What stayed the same?

Choose your favorite type of fruit and set aside some time to really savor eating it. Start by observing its physical characteristics with your eyes. Smell its fragrance and experience how it feels in your hands. Lift the fruit to your mouth slower than usual, and feel it land on your lips and tongue. Taste the fruit as if for the first time and chew 30 times before you swallow. Listen to the sound it makes in your mouth. Notice the quality of your thoughts that arise as you eat.

How does this experience compare to the way you usually eat?

Imagine that your body has a voice and could tell you its history.
What would it want to say?

I am your body and this is my story. It all started when…

_____
_____
_____
_____
_____
_____
_____
_____
_____
_____
_____
_____

What I need from you now is…

_____
_____
_____
_____
_____
_____
_____
_____
_____
_____
_____
_____
_____
_____

Your thoughts impact your body and your body impacts your thoughts.

Describe a time in the recent past when your mind influenced how you
felt in your body.

Describe a time in the recent past when your body influenced your thoughts.

How will being mindful of your mind-body connection help you
manage future stress?

compassion invites us to open our heart
to everyone who experiences joy and
loss, pleasure and pain, hope and
despair. this includes ourselves.

compassion and forgiveness

Compassion is an active attempt to offer kindness and care to what hurts, with an understanding that not everything can be fixed. Forgiveness is a radical act of compassion that frees us from the burdens of shame, hatred, and delusion. These are the ultimate acts of self-care.

Write about a time when you were kind to another person.

Write about a time when you were kind to yourself.

Is it usually easier for you to be kind to yourself or to someone else
and why do you think that is?

In what ways do you use self-criticism as a motivator?

What are some kinder alternatives that will motivate you from a place of
self-compassion so you can be your best self?

Sit comfortably or lie down where you will be at ease. Spend a few moments and several rounds of breath for each item:

1. Notice how your body feels as you begin this exercise. Notice your mood, areas of tension, the quality of your breath.

2. Imagine seeing yourself through the eyes of someone who loves you unconditionally. This could be a real person, an imagined being, or even a pet.

3. Place your hand over your heart or wrap your arms around yourself as though giving yourself a hug. Experience what it is like to hold yourself with tenderness.

4. Silently offer yourself words of kindness, such as "I care about you," "I love you," "Your grief matters to me," or "May I be free from suffering."

5. Notice if there is anything else you want to say to yourself, and speak it silently or out loud.

How did your body feel at the start of this exercise and how do you feel now?

What words of kindness did you say to yourself?

Who are the people that you can count on when you need support?
Include any organizations, such as your local hospice, support group,
crisis hotline, or cause-oriented charity, that you find helpful.

Is there anyone else or are there any other organizations you would like to add
to your support network? Make a list here, and commit to reaching out to one
or two over the next week.

start your day with self-compassion

Small changes to how you relate to yourself can have a significant impact on your well-being and ability to navigate grief. A few minutes of self-compassion in the morning sets the tone for the day so you can address difficult emotions skillfully and remember to replace self-criticism with self-kindness.

Before you get out of bed each day, spend a minute or two being kind to yourself. There are countless ways you can do this. Here are a few ideas to get you started:

- Place your hand over your heart, and feel your breath rise and fall as you offer yourself kind and gentle words.
- As you imagine your day ahead, consider how you can support yourself during any foreseen difficult moments. Consider how you can take care of yourself before, during, and after any difficult meetings or tasks.
- Plan one kind thing you're going to do for yourself later that day.
- Give yourself a shoulder or foot massage as you acknowledge your basic human goodness.

Create a list of your own ideas to wake up with self-compassion.

_____

_____

_____

_____

_____

_____

_____

_____

_____

_____

TIP: Put a sticky note on your alarm clock or a reminder in your smart phone to help you commit to this daily practice!

be your own best friend

Acceptance in the mindful context means that even when the unthinkable happens, we honor our self and our experience with dignity and kindness. Rather than turn our back on our own suffering, we treat ourselves as we would a beloved friend. We take the time to pay attention to the physical sensations, thoughts, and feelings that accompany our pain.

Imagine you have a beloved friend who is going through **exactly** what you are going through right now. Knowing you cannot change the circumstances, what would you say to help them feel understood, loved, and supported if they came to you seeking comfort and care?

Read the words you just wrote out loud to yourself, slowly and with feeling. What is it like to receive this type of support from yourself?

Go for a walk or to a place where you can observe people from a distance. Without letting anyone know what you are doing, silently and to yourself offer these words to the people you see:

May you be happy as I wish to be happy.
May you know peace as I wish to know peace.
May you be free from suffering, as I wish to be free from suffering.

What impact does this activity have on how you feel about your connection to other people?

Do you think sending silent well wishes to others will impact their life? Note any observations about the other people during the activity.

Choose someone you find a **little** challenging to be around, but who is not someone who has caused you great harm. Imagine offering them these same words of compassion from page 52.

How does this activity change or reinforce the way you feel about this person?

_____
_____
_____
_____
_____
_____
_____
_____
_____
_____
_____

What impact does this activity have on the way you feel about yourself?

_____
_____
_____
_____
_____
_____
_____
_____
_____
_____
_____
_____
_____
_____

Think of a person who has experienced the same loss as you. How is your experience of grief similar? How is it different?

What is one action you can take over the next week to offer compassion to this person, either directly or privately without them knowing?

Your loss is very personal. There are also people around the globe who are in similar circumstances. Acknowledging that you are not the only one in the world with this type of suffering can make you feel more connected and less lonely and afraid.

1. Inhale as you offer yourself compassion for the one thing that causes you the most significant amount of suffering right now.
2. Exhale as you radiate out the same compassion to everyone in the world suffering in the same way as you.
3. Do this for several minutes until you feel a sense of connection in your body and heart.

What did you choose to focus on for this practice, and how did acknowledging the universality of loss influence the way you feel towards other people?

How did it influence the way you feel towards yourself?

Forgiveness is something you do for yourself. It is a letting go; a shift in your perspective. It does not mean that you deny your pain, just as you do not choose anger as your identity.

Reflect on a time you caused harm to yourself. In the space below, ask for and offer yourself forgiveness.

Reflect on a time you caused harm to another person. In the space below, ask for and offer yourself forgiveness.

Forgiveness does not always come quickly. If you are open to the possibility that you can forgive and be forgiven, make it a practice. Remember that practice does not have to be perfect—we just have to try.

Reflect on a time when a person who is alive though no longer in your life caused you harm. In the space below, offer them your forgiveness.

_____

_____

_____

_____

_____

_____

_____

_____

_____

_____

_____

Reflect on a time when a person who died or is no longer in your life caused you harm. In the space below, offer them your forgiveness.

_____

_____

_____

_____

_____

_____

_____

_____

_____

_____

_____

A mind map is a simple diagram to ignite your creativity and visually organize ideas around an initial concept. Use the template below to brainstorm ideas about compassion. Fill in existing circles, and add new ones until the idea feels fully developed. Tap into your mindful presence and allow the words to flow freely and without judgment.

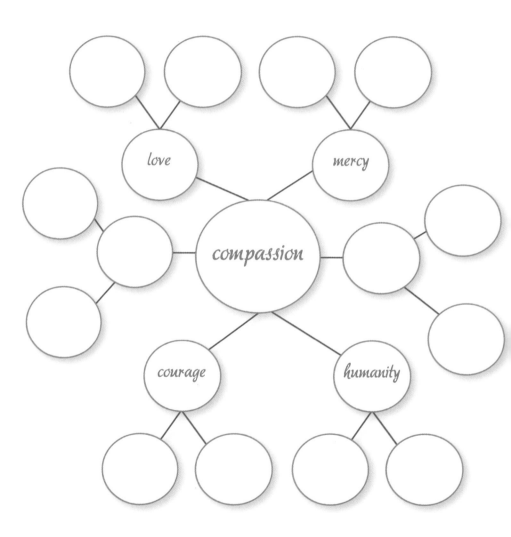

Choose a few words from your mind map on page 58 and create six phrases about compassion with these words.

1.

2.

3.

4.

5.

6.

Using the phrases above for inspiration, write a short poem that conveys the essence of compassion.

skillful courage is the strength
to face our pain and the wisdom
to honor our vulnerability.

skillful courage

Doing something even when you are afraid is the definition of courage. Skillful courage adds in a layer of wisdom that empowers us to harness our strengths and vulnerabilities so we can cope with grief and start to reengage with life after loss.

What does vulnerability feel like in your physical body?

What does strength feel like in your physical body?

Our subconscious body language can convey how we're feeling inside, but we can also alter how we're feeling by consciously changing our body language and position. Mindfully scan through your body and focus your attention on your breath for a few moments. After each step below, spend a few minutes savoring what you feel before moving onto the next step:

1. Move into a position that represents vulnerability to you.
2. Next, move into a position that represents strength to you.
3. Move back and forth between the two positions four times.
4. During the last round, pause halfway between the two positions.

Describe how the first position represents vulnerability.

_____

_____

_____

_____

_____

Describe how the second position represents strength.

_____

_____

_____

_____

What stood out to you when you paused between the two?

_____

_____

_____

_____

_____

Describe something you were afraid to do but did anyway and what
you learned from the experience.

How does the above experience relate to how you are experiencing grief?

What I really want those who care about me to know is…

RAIN meditation for difficult emotions

Difficult emotions are powerful messengers that let you know something isn't right. The discomfort you feel is a signal for you to slow down and tend to what hurts, but all too often we either turn away or intensify our pain. The RAIN meditation is a four-step process that invites you to mindfully observe the physical sensation of emotion with equanimity—a calm and steady mind. This frees you from erroneous thoughts and creates space for compassion, wisdom, and insight.

1. **RECOGNIZE** the emotion and name it: fear, sadness, vulnerability, confusion, blame, shame, anger, etc.

2. **ALLOW** the feeling to unfold with a sense of calm abiding, if it feels safe to observe it mindfully. If you do not feel safe, do not force the practice, but do whatever you need to do to take care of yourself in this moment.

3. **INVESTIGATE** the physical feeling of the emotion in your body.

- Where do you feel the emotion lives in your body?
- What is the size and shape of the emotion?
- Does it have a temperature, a color?
- What is the emotion made of on the outside? The inside?
- Is the emotion static? Pulsing? Moving in any way?
- Are there tense places in the rest of your body that you can release?

4. **NURTURE** yourself with self-compassion and kindness. Offer yourself compassion through words or actions. For example, gently stroke your face, make yourself a cup of tea, or repeat to yourself, "May I be free from this suffering."

This week when a difficult emotion arises, practice RAIN and describe how that feels.

_____

_____

_____

_____

_____

_____

_____

_____

_____

dual process model of coping
with bereavement

Most of us naturally oscillate back and forth between tending to grief and relearning how to live our day-to-day life (Stroebe & Schut, 1999). We attend to our grief by focusing on our loss: looking at photos, crying, missing someone deeply, and even dealing with the paperwork they left behind. Restoration-oriented activities, such as working, watching a funny movie, exercising, and meeting up with friends, remind us that we can still live even after our loss.

Ways I focus on my loss

Ways I go on living

Describe a time when you felt you needed to appear strong, but you did not feel strong.

_____

_____

_____

_____

_____

_____

_____

_____

_____

_____

How did you feel afterwards?

_____

_____

_____

_____

_____

_____

_____

_____

_____

_____

_____

_____

In what way could being afraid of appearing weak cut you off from other people?

In what way could being afraid of appearing weak cut you off from yourself?

Describe a recent experience where you were open and vulnerable
to another person. Did it deepen your connection?

Describe a recent experience where you were open and vulnerable to
yourself. Did it change how you view yourself?

I am able to be myself when…

Reflect on the above and read your words aloud. Is there anything getting in the way of this right now?

Imagine that the vulnerable part of you is a small child in need of care. Write an encouraging letter to yourself that you would love to receive.

Reflect on the many ways you have supported yourself since your loss—from taking care of your most basic needs to overcoming seemingly insurmountable challenges. Write your inner strength a thank-you letter. You may also include a request for future support to your inner strength in your letter.

If the tension in your body is like a suit of armor, what is it protecting?

_____

_____

_____

_____

_____

_____

_____

_____

What would it be like to take your suit of armor off once in a while?

_____

_____

_____

_____

_____

_____

_____

_____

What would it be like to put your suit of armor away for good?

_____

_____

_____

_____

_____

_____

_____

_____

_____

When I am able to accept myself just as I am, I feel...

the path of grief is not a straight line;
it is meandering and full of switchbacks.

getting unstuck

Difficult emotions are powerful messengers, alerting you that something is out of balance. Although you may feel like you are stuck in your grief, encountering these roadblocks is all part of the journey. Learning how to navigate them with compassion instead of resistance will free you from their constraints.

According to classic Buddhism, there are five mental hindrances that are common roadblocks that get in the way of our ability to be present, both on and off the meditation cushion. Just being aware these exist can be helpful, as can having compassion for yourself when they arise. For each hindrance that you are encountering in your life right now, make a few notes about what you observe when it appears.

Sensual desire/craving/greed:

Aversion/hatred/ill-will:

Physical and mental exhaustion:

Restlessness/anxiety/worry:

Doubt/hopelessness:

Which of the five hindrances on the opposite page is most noticeable in your life right now and how is it impacting your life, including your relationships, your work, and how you care for yourself?

_____

_____

_____

_____

_____

_____

_____

_____

_____

_____

_____

_____

_____

How would your life be different without it?

_____

_____

_____

_____

_____

_____

_____

_____

_____

_____

_____

_____

Physically, the edge is the place in a stretch or yoga posture that is not too much and not too little. You are not bored; neither are you causing yourself harm. The emotional edge is very similar. It is a place where you can observe your experience with a sense of calm abiding and openness.

Using this exercise below, explore how you physically relate to the edge:

1. Sit comfortably on the floor or on a chair with your eyes closed or softly focused on a point in front of you.
2. Facing forward and with your shoulders level and torso straight, tilt your head to the right as far as it will go without strain.
3. Reach your right arm up to the ceiling, and bend your elbow so your right hand rests on your left ear.
4. Create a gentle stretch on the left side of your neck using your arm, pause when you reach your edge.
5. Notice your breath and your body, and pause here for a few moments.
6. Repeat this exercise on the other side.

Is your experience with the edge in your body similar or different to how you relate to your emotional edges and in what ways?

When I am mindful of how I really feel without judging my experience, I am...

savoring the good

Appreciating the little things that bring you pleasure throughout your day can reverse your brain's natural tendency to cling to negative experiences and forget about the positive ones. (Hanson, 2016). Choose one day this week to follow the three-step process below. If you decide to do this every day, your brain will rewire itself to focus more on what is going right rather than what is wrong.

1. Seek out six positive experiences today. From a good cup of coffee or the feeling you get when you listen to music you love, there are many opportunities to pay attention to the little positives.

2. Turn up the volume and really enjoy the experience. Try to stay with the feeling for 20–30 seconds. Let this be an embodied experience, imagining that positivity fills up every cell of your being.

3. Soak it in and intend for it to work. Hold this positive sensation in your awareness, knowing that it is helping your brain rewire itself for resilience and peace.

1.

2.

3.

4.

5.

6.

transform your life with gratitude every day

In addition to the on-the-spot practice of Savoring the Good, taking a few minutes in the morning and at night to practice gratitude can help you see the world in a more positive light. Gratitude also has a powerful impact on your physical and mental health. Even when things are not going well, appreciating the gift of **this** moment, for clean drinking water, or for your ability to express how you feel in your journal, can create some space for you to move forward in your life, one little step at a time. Try the following practices:

MORNING PRACTICE

My intention for today is:

_____

_____

Today I am grateful for:

_____

_____

EVENING PRACTICE

Today I felt:

_____

_____

Today I savored:

_____

_____

Today I learned:

_____

_____

My intention for tomorrow is:

_____

_____

If you enjoyed this practice, add it to your daily self-care ritual.

If you could go back in time, what do you wish you had done
or said before the loss?

How will you feel when you make peace with this regret?

Is there something you wish someone had said to or done for you before the loss?

Is there something you wish someone had said to or done for you after the loss?

What activities, people, or thoughts drain your physical energy?

What activities, people, or thoughts drain your mental energy?

Do you notice a connection between the above?

One thing I have the power to take care of in my life right now is...

_____

_____

_____

_____

_____

_____

_____

_____

_____

I will start doing this on this date:

_____

After you have taken this step, write your reflection here.

_____

_____

_____

_____

_____

_____

_____

_____

_____

_____

_____

_____

_____

Make a list of things you can do to calm yourself when you feel anxious.

Are there additional calming techniques you can explore? Keep an on-going list here.

My greatest hope for myself over the next few months is…

A mandala is a circular design that has repeating colors, shapes, and patterns that radiate out from the center and are often created to aid spiritual growth and reflection, but can also be a way to relax your body and mind through meditative drawing. Create your own mandala with colored pens or pencils using the template below. Relax, stay connected to your breath, and move as slowly as you need to in order to stay present. When you notice your mind thinking, invite it back to drawing.

1. Decorate one section in the center of the inner most circle.
2. Repeat this in each of the center sections until the inner circle is filled.
3. Working from the center towards the outside, repeat the first two steps for each circle.

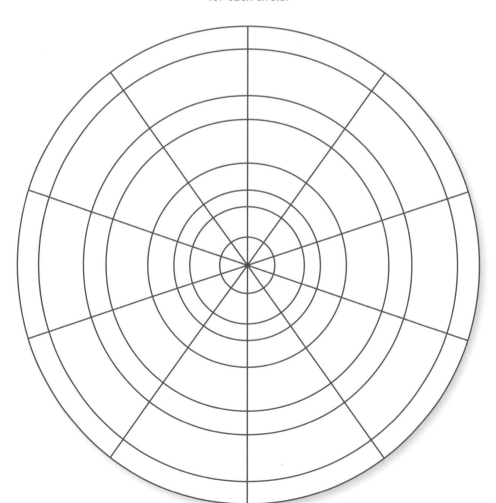

Write yourself two permission slips.

This is for something you give yourself permission to do:

I give _____
                              [YOUR NAME]

permission to _____

_____
                              [ACTIVITY]

on _____
                       [DATE OR TIME PERIOD]

so that _____

_____
                  [DESIRED OUTCOME OR FEELING]

signature _____ date _____

This is for something you give yourself permission **not** to do (at least for now):

I give _____
                              [YOUR NAME]

permission to NOT _____

_____
                              [ACTIVITY]

on _____
                       [DATE OR TIME PERIOD]

so that _____

_____
                  [DESIRED OUTCOME OR FEELING]

signature _____ date _____

fortunately, most of us possess a natural resilience, and are able, eventually, to reorient ourselves and live a meaningful life once more.

meaning reconstruction

As painful as grief and loss are, humans are wired to survive. The challenges you face and overcome will teach you new ways to take care of yourself, greet others with compassion, and adjust to your new worldview. Eventually you will live a life full of meaning and coherence once more.

What philosophical or spiritual beliefs have influenced your grief experience?

Have those philosophical or spiritual beliefs changed in any way since your loss?

The ways I have changed since my loss include...

Go for a leisurely, extended walk outside, or find a place where you can sit and do nothing for a little while. Be aware of your breath, body, and sensory experience most of the time, but allow your mind to wander a little bit.

Describe how you stay connected to yourself.

_____

_____

_____

_____

_____

_____

_____

_____

_____

_____

_____

_____

Describe how you stay connected to the person who died.

_____

_____

_____

_____

_____

_____

_____

_____

_____

_____

_____

_____

_____

_____

Remembering or revising what really matters to you is an essential step in meaningfully re-engaging with life after loss. Make a list of important things to you, big and small, but this time, write with your non-dominant hand. This slows you down so you can really reflect, ignites your creativity, taps into your intuition, and helps you explore your feelings, among other things.

What really matters to me…

post-traumatic growth

Although you would prefer to have your life as it was before, the reality is that grief and loss transform you. They force you to develop new skills and reconstruct how you view the world, yourself, and the people around you. Positive changes forged in the wake of tragedy are called post-traumatic growth, and fall under five domains:

increased sense of personal strength

•

awareness of new possibilities

•

improved compassion for one's self and others

•

appreciation for life in general

•

spiritual change or growth

This does not happen overnight, and not everyone experiences all five. Be patient and kind to yourself wherever you are on the journey. Know that eventually you will rebuild your shattered worldview and create a meaningful and coherent life that you can live with (Calhoun & Tedeschi, 2014).

reflect on your new worldview

Which element of post-traumatic growth resonates with you the most?

How do your thoughts, words, and deeds demonstrate this quality in you now?

How will this help you move forward?

What do you have in common with the person who died?

Personality:

_____

_____

_____

Mannerisms and features:

_____

_____

_____

Work and hobbies:

_____

_____

_____

How I view myself:

_____

_____

_____

How I view others:

_____

_____

_____

Values and beliefs:

_____

_____

_____

_____

What hobby, cause, vocation, or principle mattered most to them?

Use the space below to brainstorm different ways you can honor your loved one's memory. This can include a public event or charity, private ritual, or a collaborative project for the people closest to you and the person who died. Think of this as a research project that you can implement now or at a later date.

One thing I miss from before my loss is…

One thing I don't miss since my loss is…

What would your life be like today if the loss had not happened?

What is different in your life now because the loss did happen?

Imagine that you are the main character in a book or movie about your loss and write a plot summary for inside the book jacket or movie trailer. Write as if you are a compassionate narrator describing the main character's experience. Instead of using "I" or "me" and the first-person point-of-view, use the third person point-of-view and the pronouns "he," "she," or "they," and your name as you write.

Choose your favorite picture from before the loss that includes
at least two people or animals.

Who is in the picture?

What is their mood?

Who took this picture and why did they take it (if you know)?

Where was this picture taken?

What is in the background of the picture?

Are there any interesting physical objects in this image?

Why did you choose this picture?

Did this exercise change or reinforce how you feel about this picture now
compared to before?

Before everything changed, I believed the world was basically...

Now I believe the world is...

the goal of your transformation is to
be able to live with your loss and still
embrace the fullness of your life.

allowing transformation

There is no question that grief changes you, often in unexpected ways. And though you would never have chosen this path, you may be surprised to find that in some ways you have changed for the better. Adversity is the single path that leads to post-traumatic growth.

Keeping your hand moving at a steady pace and without editing, fill in the blanks below. Do not worry about what you write. It is OK to repeat yourself. Let this be meditative, free from judgment, and with awareness of your breath and your body.

I am

I am

I am

I am

I am

I am

I am

I am

I am

I am

I am

I am

I am

I am

I am

Read through your "I am" list and consider what is most true, and why?

Read through the list again. What is less true, and why?

Spread out a blanket or yoga mat and spend 5 to 10 minutes on the floor, stretching your body, rolling around, massaging tense muscles, or anything else that feels good and relaxing. Spend another 10 to 20 minutes inviting your body and mind to rest using the steps below:

1. Lie on your back on the floor or on your bed.
2. Unfold your arms so they rest at your sides.
3. Relax your legs. Use a bolster or rolled-up blanket underneath your knees if that feels good.
4. Let your breath come and go freely.
5. Scan through your whole body, inviting each part to unwind and relax.

What are you holding on to?

What are you allowing to release?

Write a letter to a beloved friend, or if you are bereaved, the person who died. Tell them about everything you have learned, and the many ways you have changed.

Dear _____

I am writing to you because I have so much to say.
Since I last saw you, I am aware that...

special day planner

Anniversaries. Birthdays. The Day Everything Changed (sometimes known as an Angelversary or Deathversary). These often trigger a tsunami of anxiety, sadness, and even fear. As with many things in life, planning ahead can go a long way to ease anticipation and make you feel more in control. Use the reflections below to transform the most dreaded days into a sacred opportunity for connection, remembrance, and honoring love.

I am planning a special day in honor of _____

on [date] _____

What types of grief reactions do you anticipate or are you already experiencing?
Include physical, emotional, social, and behavioral responses.

_____

_____

_____

_____

_____

What are a few skillful ways you can redirect your attention or distract yourself
if you feel overwhelmed?

_____

_____

_____

_____

_____

What are the most important things you will remember and acknowledge
on this special day?

_____

_____

_____

_____

_____

What types of rituals, actions, or new traditions will you implement
to honor this special day?

_____
_____
_____
_____
_____

Are there any physical objects you want to have with you?

_____
_____
_____
_____
_____

Who do you want to connect with? Who do you want to avoid?

_____
_____
_____
_____
_____

What will you say to yourself to cultivate an attitude of self-compassion
on this special day?

_____
_____
_____
_____
_____

Choose a power anthem, a song that makes you feel strong and resilient. Listen, and sing along and move your body if that feels right to you.

What is your favorite line from this song?

How does this song reflect who you are in the process of becoming?

Most superheroes have a back story full of personal loss and adversity that motivates them to save the planet. While each is known for their superhuman strength, they also exhibit vulnerabilities. Use the space below to describe your inner superhero.

My superhero name is...

_____

_____

_____

_____

My superpowers are...

_____

_____

_____

_____

_____

_____

_____

_____

My life's mission is...

_____

_____

_____

_____

_____

_____

_____

_____

_____

List the new roles in your life you have taken on since the loss and how that feels.

List the roles in your life you have released because of the loss and how that feels.

What is something that you really want to try but haven't yet?

What is holding you back?

Set a date in the future to start doing it:

Include the details of how you plan to do it here.

The hardest thing I had to do since my loss is…

The thing I am most proud of about myself since the loss is...

Make a list of the tools, techniques, and support systems that help you cope with your loss. Consider all the people, practices, books, places, animals, objects, and events that allow you to start living your life again.

What surprises me the most about myself now is…

mindfulness is called a "practice"
because it doesn't have to be perfect.
isn't that a relief?

perpetual mindfulness

You will never forget your loss, but you will survive and maybe even thrive. However, there will be times when the pain reappears. Mindfulness is your refuge in difficult times and will help you to savor the moments in between. Mindfulness is not just another coping skill or a way to improve your physical and mental health. Mindfulness is a way of being that empowers you to live and love fully.

Being mindful means spending more of each day in the present. Yet it is so easy to time travel to the past and future! Choose one day to pay attention to how present you are, without judgment or self-criticism, of course. Just knowing that you will reflect on this in the evening will help you remember to be in the moment more often. At the end of the day, fill in the prompts below, estimating the percent of time or hours of the day you recall rehashing the past, rehearsing the future, or being present, then noting what you focused on and how you felt. Repeating this exercise every day helps boost your mindful presence.

REHASHING THE PAST

Time spent thinking about the past: _____

_____

Event most focused on: _____

_____

Physical sensations, feelings, and thoughts: _____

_____

_____

_____

REHEARSING THE FUTURE

Time spent thinking about the future: _____

_____

Event most focused on: _____

_____

Physical sensations, feelings, and thoughts: _____

_____

_____

_____

BEING PRESENT

Time spent being in the present moment:

What you noticed:

Physical sensations, feelings, and thoughts:

What is one thing you can do to be more present more often?

Sit comfortably and make a couple of circles with your neck and head, keeping your shoulders steady and noticing your breath.

Now go in the opposite direction for a couple more circles at half the speed you were before.

Next, go back the other way and slow it down, so slow that movement is barely perceptible.

When I slow things down, I am…

Set aside 15 or more minutes to sit in meditation. Spend a few minutes doing each of the following in this order:

1. Focus on just one thing—such as breath or sound—until you feel your mind has stabilized.
2. Open your awareness to allow any of your senses into your field of awareness.
3. Let go of all techniques and sit in choiceless awareness, relinquishing control of anything except noticing whatever you notice.
4. Write down whatever you are aware of using this prompt:

I am aware…

mindful maintenance in minutes every day

Just a few mindful minutes a day can boost your ability to handle all kinds of stress: from loss to work to interpersonal relationships. It will also help you get to know yourself better. The key to equanimity—a calm and steady mind—is to have a regular mindfulness practice. Even five minutes can help, especially if done several times a week. Frequency is more important than duration here. It is better to practice five minutes a day, five days a week, than one hour on a Saturday. This puts your mind into the habit of being mindful, and you can track how you regularly feel, so you know when to use your coping tools and when to add in a little extra self-care. There are two types of mindfulness practice that will help you build resilience and develop insight: formal and informal mindfulness practice.

Formal mindfulness practice includes seated and walking meditation practiced for a set duration, such as 20 minutes of mindfulness meditation, or an hour of mindful movement, such as yoga or tai chi.

Informal mindfulness practice includes countless activities that nurture focus, presence, and compassion in your everyday life. Add your ideas to the list below:

- Savor your first bite of lunch
- Pay attention to how your body feels when you are having a conversation
- Sense your fingers on the keyboard as you take a mindful breath
- _____
- _____
- _____
- _____

mindfulness practice log

Planning ahead and keeping track of your progress is the key to making mindfulness a permanent part of your life.

1. Use your personal calendar to schedule time with yourself to practice mindfulness every day, even for just a few minutes. Think of this meeting as necessary, not optional.
2. Use the Formal Meditation Practice Log to keep track of your daily meditation experience.
3. Use the Informal Meditation Practice Log to reflect on moments during the day when you remembered to be mindful, including what inspired the spontaneous awareness.

FORMAL MINDFULNESS PRACTICE LOG

Date/time	Mindfulness practice technique and reflections

INFORMAL MINDFULNESS PRACTICE LOG

Date/time	Spontaneous mindful action and reflections

A refuge is a place you go when you are in distress. If you commit to a mindful life, there is a good chance that you will struggle with your practice at some point. This was also true in ancient times. Buddhism says that we need three types of support to keep our practice grounded in truth and to help us navigate difficult times. The Three Refuges are:

- The Buddha—also thought of as buddha-nature, which is the basic goodness and potential for enlightenment in all beings.
- The sangha—a spiritual community that supports, inspires, and guides you on your journey.
- The dharma—the universal truth that while suffering is inevitable in this human existence, freedom from suffering is possible.

List your personal sources of refuge that you can turn to the next time you feel you are in distress:

Imagine you are struck by an arrow. It hurts. Then imagine being struck immediately by a second arrow. That hurts even more. The Buddha explained that the first arrow is an injury that cannot be avoided. The second arrow represents our unskillful reaction to the first: it is not an external source of pain, like the first arrow, but an internal one that we create ourselves. It escalates our initial pain into suffering.

Think of a time in the past where you added suffering onto an already painful situation.

Describe the initial pain.

_____

_____

_____

_____

_____

Describe your reaction.

_____

_____

_____

_____

_____

Knowing what you know now, and without judgment for your response at the time, how would you mindfully tend to your pain?

_____

_____

_____

_____

_____

What unskillful mental or physical habit would you like most to release?

What need does it currently serve for you?

What mindfulness techniques will help you make this change to a more skillful habit?

Describe a recent experience practicing your favorite formal or informal mindfulness technique.

If you were telling a friend why this one is your favorite, what would you say?

What will always change?

What can you always count on?

Notice the part of you that is aware that you are aware. Experience the expansive nature of your consciousness, noticing how nothing—not sight, sound, smell, touch, taste, or even thoughts and feelings—is bigger than your awareness. Sit in this mindful awareness for 10 minutes or more.

Compare how you felt when you started this journal to how you feel now.

_____

_____

_____

_____

_____

_____

_____

_____

_____

Make a list of what you noticed, experienced, or learned along the way.

_____

_____

_____

_____

_____

_____

_____

_____

_____

_____

_____

Circle one thing that stands out to you from the above list.

Reflect on what you circled on page 138:

Why does this matter?

_____
_____
_____
_____
_____
_____

What has this changed?

_____
_____
_____
_____
_____

What is the next best thing you can do for yourself to have
more (or less) of this in your life?

_____
_____
_____
_____
_____
_____
_____

Think of one or two empowering words that describe how you are now that
you have this awareness, and fill in the affirmation statement below:

I am _____
_____

when you are grieving, it can be beneficial to spend time with others and share your story of loss in a mindful way. not to relive the pain over and over, but to help you make sense of your loss and learn that you are not alone.

sharing your story
of love and loss

Helping others is a transformational experience for everyone involved. Your wisdom, compassion, and insight will give them hope and honor your ability to cope with adversity and live a life with meaning. Let your inner wisdom guide you, and when you know the time is right, use your skillful courage to embark on the next step of your healing journey.

Sharing your experience of loss and healing with your peers is an act of compassion that will help you as much as the person you support. Helping others is not something to rush into. Still, deeper insight may come from reviewing your experience through the lens of selfless service.

What is one thing that you have learned from tending to your grief mindfully that you think would help a person in a similar situation?

How would you explain it in a way that someone without your experience
would understand?

Why is this important?

resources

Thank you for spending time with me in this guided journal. Here are a few other resources for grief and loss that I hope you will find helpful:

Awaken Meditation & Journaling for Grief Online Group

Facilitated by Heather Stang at MeditationForGrief.com

The Mindfulness & Grief Podcast

Inspirational guests interviewed by Heather Stang. Listen wherever you get your podcasts.

The Mindfulness & Grief Institute

Free mindfulness-based grief resources and articles: MindfulnessAndGrief.com

Find a yoga therapist near you

Phoenix Rising Yoga Therapy practitioner directory: PRYT.com

International Association of Yoga Therapists: IAYT.org

Association of Death Education and Counseling

For all grief professionals: ADEC.org

Other books by or featuring contributions by Heather Stang

Mindfulness & Grief: With Guided Meditations to Calm Your Mind and Restore Your Spirit (CICO Books, 2018)

Superhero Grief: The Transformative Power of Loss (Routledge, 2020)

Intimacy and Sexuality During Illness & Loss (Hospice Foundation of America, 2020)

Techniques of Grief Therapy: Assessment & Intervention (Routledge, 2016)

Feeling overwhelmed? Help is a call away:

National Suicide Prevention Hotline (US): 1-800-273-8255

Canada Suicide Prevention Service: 1-833-456-4566

Samaritans Suicide Prevention Hotline (UK): 116 123

references

Page 66: The RAIN acronym was first coined by mindfulness teacher Michelle McDonald.

Page 67: Stroebe, M.S., and Schut., "The Dual Process Model of Coping with Bereavement," *Death Studies*, 23, pp. 197–224 (1999)

Page 82: Hanson, R., *Hardwiring Happiness* (Harmony, 2016)

Page 98: Calhoun, L.G., and Tedeschi, R.G., *Handbook of Posttraumatic Growth* (Lawrence Erlbaum Associates, 2006)